CLIMBING ROSES

CLIMBING ROSES

AN ILLUSTRATED GUIDE TO VARIETIES, CULTIVATION AND CARE, WITH
STEP-BY-STEP INSTRUCTIONS AND OVER 160 BEAUTIFUL PHOTOGRAPHS

Andrew Mikolajski

Consultant: Lin Hawthorne
Photography by Peter Anderson

southwater

This edition is published by Southwater
an imprint of Anness Publishing Ltd
Blaby Road, Wigston, Leicestershire LE18 4SE
info@anness.com

www.southwaterbooks.com; www.annesspublishing.com

If you like the images in this book and would like to investigate
using them for publishing, promotions or advertising, please visit
our website www.practicalpictures.com for more information.

A CIP catalogue record for this book is available from the British Library.

Publisher: Joanna Lorenz
Senior Editor: Clare Nicholson
Designer: Michael Morey
Production Controller: Pirong Wang

PUBLISHER'S NOTE
Although the advice and information in this book are believed to be accurate and true at the time
of going to press, neither the authors nor the publisher can accept any legal responsibility or liability
for any errors or omissions that may have been made nor for any inaccuracies nor for any loss,
harm or injury that comes about from following instructions or advice in this book.

Contents

Introduction

*F*ew sights in the garden can compare with that of a climbing rose at the height of its glory. Each year at around summer's peak – and sometimes again later – the climbing roses put on a breath-taking display that is unmatched by any other group of plants. Many scent the air for some distance around them.

Climbing roses are multi-talented. They can embrace a conifer or an ancient oak tree, cover a wall or be trained to twine around a pergola to create a bower of flowers. They are also excellent for blocking or hiding unwanted views, such as an ugly shed or garage. There are some modern climbers that can be grown in containers and enjoyed in even the tiniest garden. This book shows you how to care for these versatile plants and illustrates some of the most beautiful available.

■ RIGHT
The rambling rose 'Seagull' seen here framing a vista at the height of summer.

The history of climbing roses

Climbing roses are a disparate group of plants that share no common ancestor. The term "climbing rose" is usually understood to include rambling roses (often with large trusses of small flowers produced in a single flush in mid-summer) as well as true climbing roses that tend to flower recurrently. Ramblers generally produce masses of very flexible canes and flower on year-old wood; climbers, often more stiffly upright, flower on new wood (for details see Growth habits and flower shapes).

In the wild, few roses are natural climbers, but there are several that make huge, scrambling shrubs with long, flexible stems that are described botanically as scandent (ascending or loosely climbing). Such roses rapidly colonize any shrub or tree that impedes their progress by attaching themselves to the host plants by means of their sharp, hooked thorns.

Many climbing roses grown in gardens today have the Chinese species *Rosa gigantea* in their ancestry. As its name suggests, this is an enormous plant that can reach a height and spread of 16.5m (54ft) or more. Fortunately, most modern climbing roses are more restrained. Many rambling roses have been derived from *R. wichurana*, a species found in Japan, Korea, China and Taiwan, that has lax stems that either trail or climb. The evergreen European *R. sempervirens* has also played a part, as has the Japanese *R. multiflora*. *R. luciae*, similar to *R. wichurana*, has played a minor role.

Some climbing roses are sports (spontaneous mutations) of bush roses. A climbing sport can be recognized by having "Climbing" in its name, for example, 'Climbing Peace', 'Climbing Blue Moon' and 'Climbing Queen Elizabeth'.

■ OPPOSITE

The rambling rose 'Bleu Magenta' bears
its flowers in clusters, as does one of its
parents, the vigorous *R. multiflora*.

■ BELOW

An archetypal cottage garden rose,
'Zéphirine Drouhin' has the advantage
of thornless stems.

Some of the old-fashioned
Bourbon roses, such as 'Louise Odier'
and 'Madame Isaac Pereire', both
of which have long, flexible stems,
can also be grown as climbers,
as can some of the China roses.

Although roses have been popular
garden plants for centuries, interest in
the breeding of new varieties of
climbing rose declined between
the two World Wars. This lack of
popularity was possibly due to the
climbing rose's need for regular
maintenance and the fact that many
flowered only once. (A neglected
climber can become a menace,
making impenetrable thickets of
tough, thorny stems.) As a result,
with a few exceptions, most of the
climbing roses grown in gardens
today were bred after 1949. The two
rose breeders who did most to revive
interest in breeding climbing roses
were Sam McGredy in Great Britain

■ OPPOSITE
The magnificent 'Climbing Iceberg'
is a good choice for clothing a wall,
where its flowers look most graceful.

■ BELOW
'Albertine', one of the best-loved rambling
roses of all time, at the height of its glory
in mid-summer.

and Wilhelm Kordes in Germany.
Both concentrated on shorter
growing varieties that were easier to
manage. Breeders in the USA also
made an important contribution,
especially Dr Walter Van Fleet,

who developed roses that could
survive a cold North American
winter. He bred the pink climber
that bears his name, although today
its repeat-flowering sport, 'New
Dawn', has superseded it.

More recently, a number of
"miniature" climbers have been
introduced. These have small flowers
and grow no more than 2.1m (7ft).
They are ideal for the smaller garden
or for growing in containers.

Climbing roses in the garden

There are few more idyllic images than that of a country cottage in high summer, with roses arching over the gate and covering the walls of the house. Town-dwellers can recreate this effect too. A climbing rose will lend an air of timelessness and maturity, even to the most modern home. Choose one of the heavily scented varieties, such as 'Albertine', 'New Dawn' or 'Zéphirine Drouhin'. Their scent will be especially appreciated near an open window. 'Zéphirine Drouhin' is particularly well suited for growing around a door because it has no thorns to catch on the clothing of passers-by.

Climbing roses have a number of other uses in the garden. Where there is space, you could allow the rose to grow with the minimum of pruning

■ BELOW
A climbing rose trained along a rope
in a catenary or curve looks delightful.

■ BELOW
Clematis 'The President' makes a sensational clash with the
brilliant scarlet climbing rose 'Danse du Feu'.

to produce a huge fountain of flowers. The rambling 'Albertine', grown in this way, makes a magnificent 6m (20ft) high shrub, and is one of the glories of the mid-summer garden.

'Albertine' and some other ramblers are available as weeping standards, grafted on to 1.2–1.8m (4–6ft) stems of *R. canina* or *R. rugosa*, so that you can create a cascade of flowers even in a confined area.

Climbing roses also look stunning grown over pergolas. Rustic poles are appropriate in cottage gardens, although brick pillars linked by wooden beams may last longer.

You can also train roses on ropes slung between two uprights to create garlands of flowers, called a catenary, at the back of a border. For this purpose, choose a medium-growing variety with long, flexible stems, such as 'Madame Grégoire Staechelin' that can be looped around the rope to produce festoons of flowers. Shorter-growing types, such as 'Golden Showers' or 'Handel', or one of the Bourbon roses, such as 'Madame Isaac Pereire' or 'Louise Odier', can be planted in the border and trained against pillars or tripods. Another possibility is to erect free-standing trellis panels. Train the roses against these to make a barrier that will be covered in flowers in summer but open in winter.

Rampant roses that grow up to and over 12m (40ft) high are best accommodated in most gardens by allowing them to scramble through trees, but take care to choose a

■ LEFT
A climbing or rambling
rose can make a spectacular
impression if grown up a tree.

■ BELOW
The banana-scented 'Seagull'
wings its way through a large
mature conifer.

suitably robust host plant that will be able to take the weight of the fully grown rose. Large conifers planted principally for winter interest are good candidates. An old orchard of apple or cherry trees would look enchanting wreathed in climbing roses that form great crinolines of flowers about the branches. Although this is a spectacular way of growing roses such as 'Climbing Cécile Brünner', 'Seagull' or 'Albéric Barbier', bear in mind that the vigour of the rose must be matched to the size of the tree. A large vigorous rambler will very soon smother a small tree, eventually leading to its demise.

Climbing roses can also be grown informally, but effectively, by allowing them to ramble through shrubs, such as lilacs, which are dull after their show of flowers in late spring. This is a form of wild gardening, since a strict pruning regime in such a situation would be impractical.

You can trail a climbing rose up and over a wall to make a curtain of flowers on the other side. If you have a high garden wall, try pinning to it one of the more vigorous climbing roses, such as 'Paul's Lemon Pillar'. If the wall is in the sun for much of the day, select one of the roses that benefits from additional heat, such as 'Gloire de Dijon' or a slightly tender China rose, such as *R.* x *odorata* 'Mutabilis'.

Climbing roses combine particularly well with other climbers, such as clematis or passion flowers. You can create some enchanting colour combinations if the plants flower at the same time, or you can choose an accompanying climber that flowers before or after the rose to extend the season of interest. For instance, the rose could support an earlier-flowering *macropetala*-type clematis or a large-flowered type, such as 'The President', which would flower at the same time as the rose.

Team light colours with dark ones, combine complementaries or use shades of the same colour. The pale pink climbing rose 'New Dawn' would work equally well with the pink clematis 'Nelly Moser' or the deep purple 'Jackmanii'. Try the rich red climber 'Guinée' with the smoky pink clematis 'Purpurea Plena Elegans', or 'Golden Showers' with the rich violet clematis 'Haku-ôkan'. In a white garden, try the old climber 'Madame Alfred Carrière', which has a long flowering season and tolerates some shade, with the clematis 'Henryi'. Use white foxgloves (*Digitalis purpurea* f. *albiflora*) to provide vertical interest.

All climbing roses tend to become bare at the base in time. Mask this by underplanting with shallow-rooting perennials such as catmint (*Nepeta*), lambs' ears (*Stachys byzantina*), hostas or lady's mantle (*Alchemilla mollis*).

If you are restricted for space and have no more than a small patio garden, or even a balcony or roof garden, you can still enjoy climbing roses by choosing from one of the miniature climbers, such as 'Laura Ford' or 'Nice Day', which are easily grown in a large container such as a half-barrel (see Planting a climbing rose in a container).

Growth habits and flower shapes

Unlike bush roses, climbing roses cannot be conveniently ascribed to distinct groups. They have a variety of ancestors and varying growth habits that make them suitable for different garden uses. Habit – the way a rose (or any plant) grows – should be as important a consideration as flower colour and scent when choosing a rose for the garden but, unfortunately, is all too often overlooked. This section will help avoid some of the pitfalls.

Most climbing roses are deciduous, though a few, such as the vigorous 'Mermaid' and 'Albéric Barbier', are evergreen or semi-evergreen. In botanical and gardening terms, they are divided into ramblers and climbers.

Rambling roses

Rambling roses that are closely related to their wild ancestors, such as 'Rambling Rector', 'Seagull' and 'Wedding Day', produce large trusses of small, single, usually highly fragrant flowers in a single flush around mid-summer on slender, flexible canes. Some are extremely vigorous indeed, and must be given plenty of room.

A few rambling roses, however, such as 'Albertine', produce larger flowers, also in clusters, on stiffer, less flexible canes. All ramblers flower on wood produced the previous year. Some flower reliably on older wood. In some cases, decorative hips follow

in the autumn. After flowering, most produce large quantities of new wood from around the base of the plant. Ramblers usually need ample space to give of their best, and are suitable for informal planting in a wild garden. They do not lend themselves to formal planting schemes and are less suitable than climbers for growing against walls.

CLIMBING ROSES THAT ARE STIFFLY UPRIGHT

'Altissimo'
'Breath of Life'
'Casino'
'Climbing Mrs Sam McGredy'
'Compassion'
'Danse du Feu'
'Dreaming Spires'
'Golden Showers'
'Handel'
'High Hopes'
'Lavinia'
'Leaping Salmon'
'Maigold'
'Parkdirektor Riggers'
'Pink Perpétué'
'Ramona'
'Schoolgirl'
'Summer Wine'
'Swan Lake'
'White Cockade'

The thorny stems of the climbing rose 'Mermaid'. 'Mermaid' has single yellow flowers with wide elegant petals. No climber repeats so freely.

Rosa banksiae 'Lutea' has stems that are virtually thornless. This is the double-yellow form which carries its flowers in hanging sprays in late spring.

The very popular scented 'Rambling Rector' is extremely vigorous, and an ideal rose to grow through a tree.

Grégoire Staechelin' and 'Gruss an Teplitz', and present their flowers in elegant, nodding clusters. These varieties look good trained on pergolas, from which their flowers will hang down. Stiffly upright varieties, such as 'Handel' and 'Parkdirektor Riggers', make good pillar roses.

Most rose stems are thorny. In certain cases, as with 'Albertine' and 'Mermaid', the thorns are viciously sharp. A few varieties, however, such as 'Zéphirine Drouhin' and 'Climbing Iceberg', have virtually thornless stems.

Certain climbing roses are more shade-tolerant than bush roses,

ROSES THAT WILL TOLERATE SOME SHADE

'Albéric Barbier'

'American Pillar'

'Blush Rambler'

'Climbing Cécile Brunner'

'Félicité Perpétue'

'Goldfinch'

'Maigold'

'Madame Alfred Carrière'

'New Dawn'

'Paul's Scarlet Climber'

'Phyllis Bide'

'Veilchenblau'

Climbing roses

These usually flower twice – the first flush appearing around mid-summer, the second, lesser flush in early autumn. Some, such as 'Mermaid', have a main flush in summer followed by spasmodic flowering right up until the first frosts of winter. These flowers are produced in small trusses on the current season's growth.

It is generally desirable to train climbers to form a permanent framework of main stems, which produce flower-bearing laterals annually. This makes them suitable for formal planting schemes, and for growing on walls. Some have an arching habit, for example 'Madame

virtually flat, often revealing
prominent stamens.
Cupped
Single to fully double flowers with
curving petals, forming a shallow
to deep cup shape.
Pointed and urn-shaped
High-centred, or urn-shaped, flowers
that open from long, thin buds.

THE FOLLOWING ROSES ARE PARTICULARLY VALUED FOR THEIR STRONG SCENT

'Alister Stella Gray'
'Aloha'
'Breath of Life'
'Climbing Ena Harkness'
'Climbing Etoile de Hollande'
'Climbing Lady Hillingdon'
'Compassion'
'Gloire de Dijon'
'Guinée'
'Leaping Salmon'
'Maigold'
'Meg'
'Mermaid'
'Madame Alfred Carrière'
'Madame Grégoire Sraechelin'
'New Dawn'
'Paul's Lemon Pillar'
'Rosy Mantle'
'Schoolgirl'
'Zéphirine Drouhin'

reflecting the fact that many of the
wild roses, from which they are
descended, were woodland plants.

In response to the needs of
gardeners with only limited space,
most climbers that have been bred
since 1949 are only moderately
vigorous and in many cases grow
no more than 5m (16½ft) tall. Some
have been developed to reach only
2.3m (7½ft) or less, and miniature
climbers seldom exceed 2.1m (7ft).

Extensive breeding and cross-
breeding by modern rose breeders
have meant that all the varied flower
forms of bush roses can be found
among climbing roses, which gives
the gardener extra choice.

Flower shapes

Flat
Single (with five petals) or semi-
double (with ten) flowers that open

A semi-double flat flower.

A cupped flower.

A rounded flower.

A rosette-shaped flower.

A quartered rosette.

A pompon.

Rounded

Flowers with a rounded outline, formed by overlapping petals usually of equal size.

Rosette

Low-centred, flat flowers with many short, crowded petals.

Quartered rosette

Similar to a rosette shape, but with the petals arranged in distinctive quarters within the flower.

Pompon

Small ball-like flowers that are generally borne in clusters, with many short petals.

Left to right: Pointed and urn-shaped flowers.

Plant Directory

In the following gallery, roses are arranged alphabetically within groups as follows:

Rambling roses Usually large, rampant roses with a single, though generally spectacular, flush of flowers around mid-summer, often highly scented.

Climbing roses Usually repeat-flowering roses. They are subdivided as follows:

Large climbers Roses that reach a height of 6m (20ft) or more and are suitable for growing into trees, on large pergolas or against walls.

Medium-growing climbers Roses that do not normally exceed 5m (16½ft). They may be grown against walls and fences and on pergolas.

Shorter-growing climbers (the largest group) Roses that normally stay below 4m (13ft). Most are suitable for growing against walls and on pergolas. Many are stiffly upright and are best grown on pillars. Others, usually of recent introduction, may be grown in containers. Some roses included in this group can also be grown as shrubs if they are pruned hard.

The dimensions of height and spread given are approximate and are what the rose may be expected to achieve given good cultivation. They may vary depending on soil type, climate and season. The date the rose was first cultivated is given when known.

Rambling roses

■ ABOVE
'ALBÉRIC BARBIER'

A vigorous rambling rose, introduced in 1900. It will grow to 5m (16½ft) high and 3m (10ft) across. In early to mid-summer, it produces masses of double, rosette, creamy white, scented flowers. The leaves are glossy and often persist through the winter. 'Albéric Barbier' is a wonderful sight when in full flower, and tolerates some shade.

■ BELOW

'AMERICAN PILLAR'

A vigorous rambling rose, introduced in 1902. It will grow to 5m (16½ft) high and 2.4m (8ft) across. In mid-summer it produces clusters of reddish-pink single flowers with white centres amid glossy leaves. 'American Pillar' was a popular rose and is often found in old gardens but has fallen out of favour, perhaps because it flowers only once, lacks scent and is susceptible to mildew.

■ ABOVE

'ALBERTINE'

A vigorous rambling rose, introduced in 1921, which will grow to 5m (16½ft) high and 4m (13ft) across. The fully double, cupped, heavily scented pink flowers, borne in a single flush in mid-summer, open from copper-tinted buds; they become untidy as they age. The leaves, tinged red on emergence, are small and thick. 'Albertine' has talon-like thorns and is particularly prone to mildew in dry summers; nevertheless it remains one of the most highly rated of all ramblers due to the profusion of its flowers and their potent fragrance.

■ LEFT
'BOBBIE JAMES'

A vigorous rambling rose, introduced in 1961, which will grow to 10m (30ft) high and 6m (20ft) across. In summer it covers itself with clusters of small, white, semi-double flowers that are sweetly scented. The leaves are glossy green. 'Bobbie James' is an excellent choice for growing into a large tree. Otherwise, use only where space permits.

■ RIGHT
'RAMBLING RECTOR'

A vigorous rambling rose, introduced before 1912, which will grow to 6m (20ft) high and across. In summer it covers itself with clusters of small, single, white, fragrant flowers; small red hips follow in autumn. The leaves are glossy bright green. 'Rambling Rector', an impressive sight in maturity when in full flower, is suitable for growing into a large tree.

■ ABOVE AND INSET
'SEAGULL'

A rambling rose, introduced in 1907, which will grow to 6m (20ft) high and 4m (13ft) across. In summer it produces a single flush of clusters of small, white, single to semi-double, fragrant flowers. The leaves are greyish-green. Less vigorous than some other similar roses, 'Seagull' can be grown into a small to medium-sized tree.

■ RIGHT
'VEILCHENBLAU'

(syn. 'Blue Rambler', 'Violet Blue')
A vigorous rambling rose, introduced in 1909, which will grow to 4m (13ft) high and across. In mid-summer it produces clusters of sweetly scented, semi-double, violet-pink flowers with yellow stamens. The flowers fade to purplish-grey. The leaves are glossy and light green. More modest than most ramblers, 'Veilchenblau' is suitable for a small garden. It is best grown where there is some shelter from the midday sun.

Large climbers

■ BELOW
'CLIMBING QUEEN
ELIZABETH'

Climbing rose introduced in 1957.
Shapely, high-centred, fully double,
lightly scented, clear-pink flowers are
freely produced from summer to
autumn. The leaves are leathery and
glossy. Height 6m (20ft), spread 3m
(19ft). 'Climbing Queen Elizabeth'
is a sport of the popular shrub rose
'Queen Elizabeth'.

■ ABOVE
'CLIMBING CÉCILE BRÜNNER'

A vigorous climbing rose, introduced in 1894, which will grow to 6m (20ft) high and across.
Over a long period in summer, large clusters of small, fully double, sweetly scented, pale
pink flowers open from pointed buds. The leaves are plentiful. 'Climbing Cécile Brünner',
a sport of the dainty China rose 'Cécile Brünner', is a good choice for growing through a
tree; in other situations it can disappoint, since flowering is not always profuse.

■ LEFT

'MADAME GRÉGOIRE STAECHELIN'

A vigorous climbing rose, introduced in 1927. It will grow to 6m (20ft) high and 4m (13ft) across. In early summer fully double, rounded, sweetly scented, warm-pink flowers with slightly frilled petals are borne in profusion in hanging clusters. The leaves are matt green. 'Madame Grégoire Staechelin' flowers once only, but at its peak it can be sumptuous; it has large, showy hips that redden in autumn.

■ RIGHT

'MERMAID'

A vigorous climbing rose, introduced in 1918. It will grow to 6m (20ft) high and across. From mid-summer until autumn single, pale yellow, fragrant flowers open from pointed buds to reveal prominent golden stamens that persist after the petals have fallen. The leaves are glossy and semi-evergreen or evergreen, depending on the season; the stems are viciously thorny. 'Mermaid' tolerates some shade and is best grown where it gets shelter from hard frosts. Although the flowers are not abundant, they are beautiful.

Medium-growing climbers

■ LEFT

'CLIMBING ENA HARKNESS'

A vigorous climbing large-flowered rose, introduced in 1954. It will grow to 5m (16½ft) high and 2.4m (8ft) across. The rich scarlet, fully double, fragrant, urn-shaped flowers hang elegantly from the stems and are borne over a long period from summer to autumn. The leaves are semi-glossy. 'Climbing Ena Harkness', a sport of the bush rose 'Ena Harkness', needs a warm, sheltered site to give of its best.

■ RIGHT

'CLIMBING ICEBERG'

A climbing cluster-flowered (floribunda) rose, introduced in 1968. It will grow to 5m (16½ft) or more high and across. From summer to autumn clusters of lightly scented, creamy white, cupped, double flowers are produced among abundant, glossy light green leaves. The stems are virtually thornless. 'Climbing Iceberg', a sport of the popular shrub rose 'Iceberg', is among the most reliable of modern climbers and is a good choice for clothing a wall.

■ LEFT

'CLIMBING PEACE'

A climbing rose, introduced in 1951, and a sport of the popular large-flowered bush rose 'Peace'. It will grow to 5m (16$\frac{1}{2}$ft) high and 1.2m (4ft) across. The large, fully double, fragrant flowers are creamy yellow flushed with pink, and appear from summer to autumn. The abundant leaves are large and glossy.

■ RIGHT

'DESPREZ À FLEURS JAUNES'

(syn. 'Jaune Desprez')
A climbing noisette rose, introduced in 1830, which will grow to 5m (16$\frac{1}{2}$ft) high and across. In summer it produces fully double, quartered, fragrant, warm creamy yellow flowers that open virtually flat. The leaves are light green. Best trained against a warm wall, this rose is an exquisite climber.

■ LEFT

'GLOIRE DE DIJON'

A vigorous climbing tea rose, introduced in 1853. It will grow to 5m (16$\frac{1}{2}$ft) high and 4m (13ft) across. The striking, fully double, fragrant, quartered-rosette, buff-apricot flowers are produced over a long period from early summer to autumn. The leaves are tinged red on emergence in spring. 'Gloire de Dijon', one of the oldest climbing roses and commonly known as the old glory rose, is still widely grown; it appreciates a sunny, sheltered site.

■ BELOW

'MADAME ALFRED CARRIÈRE'

A climbing noisette rose, introduced in 1879, which will grow to 5m (16$\frac{1}{2}$ft) high and 3m (10ft) across. From summer to autumn the creamy white, double, cupped, fragrant flowers are freely produced on almost thornless stems. The leaves are large and pale green. 'Madame Alfred Carrière', a dependable rose, tolerates some shade and is excellent for growing into a tree or for covering a wall.

Shorter-growing climbers

■ ABOVE
'ALOHA'

A climbing large-flowered rose, introduced in 1949. It will grow to 3m (10ft) high and 2.4m (8ft) across. The cupped, fully double, light pink, rain-resistant flowers are borne from summer to autumn. The leaves are dark green. 'Aloha' is suitable for growing in a container.

■ ABOVE RIGHT
'BREATH OF LIFE'

A climbing large-flowered rose, introduced in 1982. It will grow to 2.4m (8ft) high and 2.1m (7ft) across. From summer to autumn it bears fully double, rounded, fragrant pink flowers. This rose can be grown as a shrub with hard pruning.

■ LEFT
'BLAIRII NUMBER TWO'

A Bourbon climber introduced in 1845. It produces an abundance of large, cupped, fully double, sweetly scented flowers in mid-summer that are pale silvery-pink with deeper pink centres. The leaves are matt dark green and rough to the touch. Height 4m (13ft), spread 2m (6^{1}/2ft). Unlike most other Bourbons, 'Blairii Number Two' will produce few, if any, further blooms in autumn.

■ ABOVE
'CASINO'

Climbing rose introduced in 1963.
Over a long period in summer the double,
fragrant, soft yellow flowers open from
pointed, deep yellow buds. The leaves
are glossy dark green. Height 3m (10ft),
spread 2.1m (7ft). 'Casino' appreciates a
warm site sheltered from cold winds. It can
be grown as a shrub with hard pruning.

■ RIGHT
'CHAPLIN'S PINK CLIMBER'

A vigorous climbing rose, introduced in
1928, which will grow to 4m (13ft) high
and 2.4m (8ft) across. From summer to
autumn it produces semi-double, lightly
scented, bright pink flowers with
prominent golden stamens. The leaves
are mid-green. It is sometimes sold as
'Chaplin's Pink'.

■ ABOVE LEFT
'CLIMBING BLUE MOON'

A climbing large-flowered rose, introduced in 1964. It will grow to 3m (10ft) high and 1.8m (6ft) across. Throughout summer it produces fully double, scented, lilac-mauve flowers that appear bluer when it is grown in full sun. The leaves are glossy green. 'Climbing Blue Moon' is a sport of the large-flowered bush rose 'Blue Moon'.

■ ABOVE RIGHT
'COMPASSION'

A climbing large-flowered rose, introduced in 1973, which will grow to 3m (10ft) high and 2.4m (8ft) across. From summer to autumn it produces shapely, rounded, fully double, sweetly scented, warm apricot-pink flowers. The leaves are dark green. 'Compassion' is excellent grown on a pillar.

■ RIGHT
'COMPLICATA'

Vigorous gallica rose, of unknown origin, suitable for training as a climber. In mid-summer it carries masses of saucer-shaped, sweetly scented, single, translucent pink flowers with white centres and golden stamens. The leaves are greyish green. Height and spread to 2.4m (8ft) or more. 'Complicata' is best suited to an informal planting, allowed to grow into trees and shrubs.

■ ABOVE LEFT
'CONSTANCE SPRY'

A shrub rose, introduced in 1961, suitable for training as a climber. It will grow to 3m (10ft) high and across. In mid-summer it produces a profusion of large, cupped, fully double, richly scented, warm-pink flowers. The leaves are coarse and greyish-green. Despite its single flush of flowers, 'Constance Spry' is one of the most desirable of modern climbers and is spectacular at its peak; it tolerates some shade.

■ ABOVE RIGHT
'CRIMSON DESCANT'

A climbing rose, introduced in 1972, which will grow to 3m (10ft) high and 1.2m (4ft) across. From summer to autumn it produces masses of double, lightly scented, bright crimson flowers. The foliage is glossy green. 'Crimson Descant' is a reliably healthy rose, tolerates some shade, and is suitable for a pillar.

■ ABOVE
'DUBLIN BAY'

A climbing rose, introduced in 1976, which has a height and spread of 2.1m (7ft). From summer to autumn clusters of double, lightly scented, almost fluorescent red flowers are produced amid healthy, glossy, large leaves. 'Dublin Bay' is a good choice where space is limited, since the growth tends to be upright.

■ ABOVE

'DANSE DU FEU'

A vigorous climbing rose, introduced in 1954, which will grow
to 2.4m (8ft) high and across. From summer to autumn it bears
clusters of double, rounded, lightly scented, luminous red flowers
among glossy, bronze-tinged, dark green leaves. 'Danse du Feu',
a popular and free-flowering rose, is prone to blackspot.

■ RIGHT

'GOLDEN SHOWERS'

A climbing rose, introduced in 1957, which will grow to 3m (10ft)
high and 1.8m (6ft) across. From summer to autumn it produces
clusters of double (but with few petals), lightly scented, yellow
flowers. The leaves are glossy dark green. 'Golden Showers'
performs well in a variety of situations and tolerates some shade.

■ LEFT
'HANDEL'

A vigorous climbing rose, introduced in 1965. It will grow to 3m (10ft) high and 2.1m (7ft) across. Double, urn-shaped, lightly scented flowers with cream petals edged with pink, are produced from mid-summer to autumn. The dark green leaves are tinged bronze. 'Handel' is valued for the unique colouring of its flowers; with hard pruning it can be grown as a shrub. Blackspot may be a problem.

■ ABOVE RIGHT
'HIGHFIELD'

A climbing rose, introduced in 1981, and a sport of 'Compassion'. It will grow to 3m (10ft) high and 2.4m (8ft) across. From summer to autumn it produces shapely, rounded, fully double, fragrant, primrose-yellow flowers. The leaves are dark green.

■ LEFT
'LAURA FORD'

A miniature climbing rose, introduced in 1990. It will grow to 2.1m (7ft) high and 1.2m (4ft) across. From summer to autumn it produces clusters of small, lightly scented, yellow flowers among small, shiny, dark green leaves. An excellent choice for a small garden, 'Laura Ford' is also suitable for growing in a container.

■ ABOVE
'LOUISE ODIER'

A Bourbon rose, introduced in 1851, suitable for training as a climber and best with some support. It will grow to 2.4m (8ft) high and 1.8m (6ft) across. From mid-summer to autumn it produces clusters of cupped, fully double, strongly scented, lilac-tinted, warm pink flowers. The leaves are greyish-green.

■ ABOVE

'MAIGOLD'

A vigorous climbing pimpinellifolia hybrid, introduced in 1953, which will grow to 2.4m (8ft) high and across. In early summer, semi-double, cupped, sweetly scented, rich-yellow flowers are produced in clusters, usually in a single flush. The leaves are leathery and glossy. 'Maigold', a tough and hardy rose, is valued for its early flowering and resistance to disease.

■ BELOW

'MORNING JEWEL'

A vigorous climbing rose, introduced in 1968, which will grow to 3m (10ft) high and 2.4m (8ft) across. Clusters of glowing-pink, double, cupped, lightly scented flowers are freely produced in mid-summer; the autumn display is less profuse. The leaves are glossy dark green. Generally a healthy rose, 'Morning Jewel' can be grown as a shrub with hard pruning.

■ LEFT

'MADAME ISAAC PEREIRE'

Bourbon rose introduced in 1881 suitable for training as a climber. From summer to autumn huge, richly fragrant, luminous cerise-pink flowers open as quartered rosettes but become muddled as they mature, especially those of the first flush. The leaves are matt, dark green. Height 2.4m (8ft), spread 2m (6½ft). 'Madame Isaac Pereire' is one of the most strongly scented of all roses. It can be prone to mildew.

■ ABOVE

'OLD BLUSH CHINA'

China rose, introduced from China around 1752 but undoubtedly much older, suitable for training as a climber. From summer to early winter, it produces double, cupped, fragrant, clear pink flowers amid elegant, pointed leaves. Height 2.4m (8ft), spread 1.5m (5ft). 'Old Blush China' rewards careful cultivation by flowering until the first frosts.

■ ABOVE

'PARKDIREKTOR RIGGERS'

A vigorous climbing rose, introduced in 1957, which will grow to 4m (13ft) high and across. From summer to autumn it produces semi-double, lightly scented, glowing crimson flowers that have prominent yellow stamens. The leaves are glossy dark green. 'Parkdirektor Riggers' is valued for its disease-resistance and long flowering season.

■ RIGHT

X *ODORATA* 'MUTABILIS'

A China rose of uncertain parentage, introduced from China some time before 1894, although it may be much older. It is suitable for training as a climber and will grow to 3m (10ft) high and 1.8m (6ft) across. The single, cupped, lightly scented flowers are borne over a long period from summer to autumn. They are of unique colouring: flame-orange in bud, they open to coppery yellow, then fade to pink, the pink deepening to purple as they age. The leaves are dark green and glossy. *R.* x *odorata* (sometimes sold as *R. chinensis* 'Mutabilis' or simply 'Mutabilis' appreciates a warm site, and in cold climates is best in full sun against a wall.

■ LEFT
'PINK PERPÉTUÉ'

A vigorous climbing rose, introduced in 1965, which will grow to 3m (10ft) high and 2.4m (8ft) across. The lightly scented flowers, which are borne from summer to autumn, are double, cupped to rosette, and have petals that are light pink with darker bases. The leaves are leathery and dark green. 'Pink Perpétué' has a spreading habit that makes it suitable for covering a wall; it can also be grown as a shrub if it is pruned hard. Rust may be a problem.

■ RIGHT
'SOMBREUIL'
(CLIMBING FORM)

Climbing rose introduced in 1850. From summer to autumn it produces flat, quartered rosette, sweetly scented flowers that are creamy white tinged with flesh pink as they age. The leaves are mid-green. Height 2.4m (8ft), spread 1.5m (5ft). The flowers of 'Sombreuil' can be spoilt by wet weather; nevertheless, it is a rose of considerable distinction.

■ BELOW
'SCHOOLGIRL'

A climbing rose which will grow to 3m (10ft) high and 2.4m (8ft) across. From summer to autumn the fully double, fragrant flowers open from urn-shaped buds. The large leaves are not plentiful. Although not free-flowering, 'Schoolgirl' is valued for its scent and unusual orange flower colour.

■ ABOVE LEFT
'SOUVENIR DE LA
MALMAISON'
(CLIMBING FORM)

Climbing rose introduced in 1893. The fully double, quartered rosette, fragrant flowers are pale pink, ageing to white, and are produced from summer to autumn. The leaves are small and dark green. Height 4m (13ft), spread 2.4m (8ft). 'Souvenir de la Malmaison' is named in honour of Empress Josephine's famous garden at Malmaison. The silk-textured flowers may be spoilt by wet weather.

■ ABOVE RIGHT
'SYMPATHIE'

A climbing large-flowered rose, introduced in 1964. It will grow to 3m (10ft) or more high and 2.4m (8ft) across. Double, fragrant, bright red flowers are produced in profusion from early summer to early autumn. 'Sympathie' tolerates some shade and is disease-resistant.

■ LEFT
'TYNWALD'

A large-flowered rose, introduced in 1979, suitable for training as a climber. It will grow to 2.4m (8ft) high and 1.2m (4ft) across. The very fragrant, creamy white flowers are shaded ivory at the centre and appear from summer to autumn. The luxuriant foliage is dark green. 'Tynwald' is a disease-resistant rose and is good for cut flowers.

■ RIGHT
'WHITE COCKADE'

A climbing rose, introduced in 1969, which will grow to 2.1m (7ft) high and 1.5m (5ft) across. Fully double, rounded, slightly scented, white flowers are produced almost continuously from summer to autumn. The dark green leaves are large and glossy. 'White Cockade' is particularly valued for its perfectly shaped flowers. It may be grown as a shrub, if pruned well, and it is a good choice for a container or growing up a short pillar.

■ LEFT
'WILLIAM LOBB'

Moss rose introduced in 1855, suitable for training as a climber. In mid-summer the large, double, rosette, heavily scented, magenta-purple flowers open from heavily mossed buds, then fade to violet-grey. The dark green leaves are produced in abundance. Height and spread 2m (6½ft). The range of tones in the flowers of 'William Lobb' as they mature and fade is remarkable.

■ ABOVE
'ZÉPHIRINE DROUHIN'

A Bourbon rose, introduced either in 1868 or 1873, which will grow to about 3m (10ft) high and 1.8m (6ft) across. During summer and autumn it produces clusters of double, cupped to flat, deep purplish-pink flowers which are strongly fragranced. The leaves are glossy light green and the stems are thornless. 'Zéphirine Drouhin', sometimes called the "thornless rose", can be grown as a shrub if it is pruned hard.

The Grower's Guide

Cultivation

Climbing roses are vigorous plants that make heavy demands on soil fertility. Good cultivation is essential if they are to give their best. Most soil types will support roses, except soil that is permanently wet. The ideal soil is an easily workable loam (made up of roughly equal parts of sand, silt and clay) that is rich in humus (decayed vegetable matter). Adding organic matter in the form of farmyard manure or garden compost improves all soil types, helping to aerate heavy soils and adding bulk and nutrients to light soils. If you have a very heavy soil, work in horticultural grit (sand) at the rate of a bucketful per sq m (sq yd) to improve the drainage.

Most climbing roses grow best in full sun. A few tolerate shade, though flowering will be less profuse. Good air circulation through the plants is important and lessens the likelihood of mildew and other fungal diseases (see Pests, diseases and other disorders). Choose a fairly open site, but with some shelter from strong winds.

For the best results, feed your roses regularly while they are in active growth. Organic and inorganic fertilizers are widely available. Using chemical fertilizers allows you to know exactly how much of the nutrient elements you are applying. Different elements produce different results. Nitrogen (N) stimulates lush, leafy growth. Potassium (K) promotes flower production. Phosphorus (P) aids root development. Balanced fertilizers (also known as straights) contain equal amounts of each, but for the optimum performance use a proprietary rose fertilizer that has a higher proportion of potassium. Organic gardeners can use pelleted chicken manure.

■ ABOVE
A fine specimen of 'Albertine' trained on a pillar, in full flower in mid-summer.

■ BELOW
A rose on a pergola produces a
cascade of flowers in summer.

When growth begins in spring, fork the fertilizer into the soil around the base of the plant at the rate recommended by the manufacturer. Water the fertilizer in well, then apply a mulch to retain moisture. Feed repeat-flowering climbers again in mid-summer immediately after deadheading (see Pruning and training), but do not feed after this, since you will encourage lush growth that will not have time to ripen fully before winter.

If your climbing roses are growing among other shrubs or against walls, where they may not receive adequate moisture and nutrients, water them regularly and spray with a foliar feed at the rate recommended by the manufacturer. Fork in a handful of bonemeal around the base of roses in the autumn to promote strong root growth. (Roots continue to grow even though top-growth has ceased.)

A new rose will not thrive in the same soil that supported another rose, even if the previous one was growing strongly (see Pests, diseases and other disorders: rose-sick soil). If you need to replace a climbing rose, remove the old plant and dig out a hole about 90cm (3ft) across and at least 45cm (1½ft) deep, and add fresh soil from another part of the garden.

Buying roses

Climbing roses are sold either as container-grown or bare-root plants. Both types eventually make equally good plants, though container-grown roses usually establish more quickly.

Bare-root plants are lifted from the open ground when dormant, and the roots are shaken free of soil. They are usually only available between autumn and early spring. Most commercial growers who sell by mail order supply their plants this way and, although there may be some delay between ordering your plants and receiving them, a huge range is available. Bare-root roses are usually despatched in specially designed padded envelopes. The roots are wrapped in a plastic bag containing peat or some similar material to keep them moist. You can store the roses unopened for up to six weeks in a dark, cool, frost-free place.

Garden centres usually prefer to sell plants in full growth in containers, but they offer a smaller choice and only the most popular varieties are likely to be available. When buying a rose in a container, look for one that is growing strongly and evenly with sturdy, well-spaced stems. To check that it is not pot-bound, slide it from its container. If the roots are congested and coil around the pot,

1 Before planting, give a bare-root rose a good soaking in a bucket of water.

2 When planting, spread out the roots as far as possible.

CHOOSING A CONTAINER-GROWN ROSE

1 Look for plants with balanced, healthy looking top-growth, without moss or liverwort on the pot's surface.

2 If possible, slide the rose gently from its container, and check that its roots are not congested.

they will continue to grow in a spiral and the plant will establish slowly.

Look for any signs of greenfly or black spot, and reject any plant that is dying back (see Pests, diseases and other disorders). The presence of a few weed seedlings on the surface of the compost is of no consequence. However, a mat of liverworts or mosses indicates that the plant has been in its pot too long and has exhausted the available nutrients.

Container-grown roses can be planted at any time of the year, except when the ground is frozen or waterlogged or during a drought in summer. Bare-root roses must be ordered in advance and planted in autumn or spring. Many gardeners find container-grown roses more convenient, but they are usually more expensive than their bare-root equivalents.

Planting a climbing rose against a wall

To grow a rose against a wall, you need to fix a trellis or system of wires to the wall. Rose thorns cannot hook on to the support itself, so you need to tie in the stems as they grow (see Pruning and training).

Mount all trellises on battens to ensure that there is adequate air circulation between the plant and the wall. This will also make it easier to remove the plant from the wall if you need to paint or repair the wall at a later date. To construct a good system of wires, use vine eyes.

Good soil preparation prior to planting is also essential if the rose is to perform as it should, and will considerably minimize maintenance later on, since the rose will need less frequent watering and feeding. Dig a good-sized hole, remove old mortar and bricks, and incorporate plenty of organic matter in the soil.

Walls cast a rain shadow: the soil at the foot of the wall does not become as wet during showers as soil in the open border, so plant the rose at least 45cm (18in) away from the wall to ensure that the roots receive adequate moisture. Angle the top growth towards the wall. During the first season, you should water the rose regularly, especially during dry spells, to ensure that it establishes well.

USING A TRELLIS

1 **Decide on the best position for the trellis on the wall, and drill holes at suitable intervals to take the battens. Tap in plugs to take the screws.**

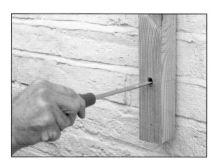

2 **Screw the battens to the wall using rust-proof screws.**

4 **Fork over the planting area, thoroughly working in organic matter (spent mushroom compost is shown here).**

3 **Check the position of the trellis, and nail it firmly to the battens.**

5 **Dig a hole at least 45cm (18in) from the wall. Fork in a handful of bonemeal at the bottom of the hole.**

6 Check the planting depth. You should aim to cover the graft union (where the top-growth is budded on the rootstock). Plant the rose so that it is just below the level of the soil.

7 Remove the rose from its pot and tease out some of the roots with a hand fork so that they will quickly grow away into the surrounding soil. This will help to accelerate establishment.

8 Position the rose in the hole, angling the top-growth towards the wall and fanning the roots out away from the wall to ensure they receive adequate moisture. Backfill with soil.

9 Firm the rose in with your foot to eliminate any pockets of air around the roots. Gently pull on a stem to check the rose is securely planted.

10 Cut back any dead or damaged growth to healthy wood, but leave longer, healthy stems unpruned. Also remove any faded flowers.

11 If the stems are long enough, fan them out horizontally and tie them loosely to the trellis. Water the rose well. If planting in spring, fork in rose fertilizer at the base of the plant.

12 *(left)* Correctly planted, the rose should quickly establish and will soon produce vigorous new shoots that can be trained to the trellis.

■ RIGHT, MIDDLE RIGHT
AND FAR RIGHT
Vine eyes hold stretched wires
to which rose stems are tied.
Screw-in vine eyes can be
used on timber or on walls
in conjunction with wall
plugs. Flat vine eyes can be
hammered into the masonry.

Using vine eyes

Vine eyes can be used when a more
flexible alternative to a trellis is
needed. Space the vine eyes about
90cm (3ft) apart horizontally and
30cm (1ft) vertically, then thread
plastic-covered wire between them.
Tie the rose stems to the wires with
soft horticultural twine or wire ties, as
they grow (see Pruning and training).

VIGOROUS ROSES SUITABLE FOR GROWING INTO TREES	
'Albéric Barbier'	'Félicité Perpétue'
'Alister Stella Gray'	R. filipes 'Kiftsgate'
'American Pillar'	'Madame Alfred Carrière'
'Blush Rambler'	R. mulliganii
'Bobbie James'	'Paul's Himalayan Musk'
'Climbing Cécile Brünner'	'Rambling Rector'
'Complicata'	'Seagull'
'Excelsa'	'Wedding Day'

Planting against a tree

If you wish to grow a rose into a
tree, you need to ensure that neither
competes unduly with the other, and
that both receive adequate moisture.
Plant the rose at least 90cm (3ft)
from the tree trunk and pay particular
attention to soil preparation. Position
the rose on the side of the prevailing
wind so it will blow the stems into
the tree as they grow.

1 Dig a hole approximately 90cm (3ft) across and 45cm (18in) deep, 90cm (3ft) from the base of the tree.

2 Add organic matter, then fork in bonemeal at the base of the hole, following the manufacturer's instructions.

3 Check the depth of the hole, then plant the rose, angling the top-growth towards the tree trunk.

4 Insert canes by the rose, then tie these to the tree. Tie the stems of the rose to the canes.

Planting a climbing rose in a container

Although the majority of climbing roses are unsuitable for growing in containers, there are several modern hybrids that make excellent plants for containers on a patio, terrace or roof garden. A number of these are listed in the panel opposite.

All miniature climbing roses can be used for this purpose. Miniature roses bear clusters of small, usually double flowers similar to those of true miniature and patio roses, and they make plants no more than 2.1m (7ft) high when grown in the open border.

When grown in a container, they are unlikely to exceed 1.5m (5ft) in height.

A climbing rose in a container can be pruned and trained in the same way as a climbing rose in the garden, but for optimum performance pay more attention to watering and feeding. Water freely during the growing season. At the height of summer you will need to water at least once, and possibly twice, a day. Feed with a rose fertilizer at the start of the season, then after the first flush of flowers. For added vigour, spray the plant regularly with a foliar feed. Do not feed after mid-summer, since this promotes sappy growth that will not ripen fully before winter and will therefore be susceptible to frost damage and may be liable to disease.

To train a climber in a container against a wall, first attach a trellis to

PLANTING A ROSE IN A CONTAINER

1 Cover drainage holes at the base of the container with stones or gravel to improve the drainage. This will also improve stability. Begin to fill the container with compost (soil mix).

2 Check the planting depth by standing the rose in its container on the compost. Make sure the graft union is covered with compost, and leave a gap of 2.5cm (1in) below the rim of the container to allow for watering.

3 Ease the rose out of its container and tease out the roots with a hand fork, so they will grow away quickly.

4 Set the rose in position in the centre of the container and begin to backfill with compost.

5 Once the correct level has been reached, firm the compost with your hands and water the rose well.

6 Insert canes or bamboos around the edge, pushing them down to the base of the container for maximum stability. An odd number of canes looks best.

7 Tie the tops of the canes together securely to create a "wigwam" over the container, or alternatively use a proprietary wigwam support.

8 Run wires or strings around the canes at intervals of about 20cm (8in), either as separate rounds or in a continuous spiral. As the rose grows, tie the stems in with wire ties or horticultural string.

9 To provide winter interest when the rose is not in bloom, plant winter pansies or underplant with ivies and a selection of dwarf spring bulbs for colour in the spring.

THE FOLLOWING CLIMBING ROSES ARE SUITABLE FOR GROWING IN CONTAINERS

'Casino'

'Céline Forestier'

'Climbing Orange Sunblaze'

'Dublin Bay'

'Golden Showers'

'Good as Gold'

'Laura Ford'

'Little Rambler'

'Maigold'

'Nice Day'

'Phyllis Bide'

'Swan Lake'

'Warm Welcome'

'White Cockade'

the wall (see Planting a climbing rose against a wall). Halved half-barrels made of wood are particularly suitable for this purpose, since they have flat backs and can be stood directly against the wall.

If you wish your rose to be a free-standing feature that can be moved around at will, train it on a wigwam of canes, as illustrated above.

Choose a container large enough to allow for a good root run. Stability is important, so the container should be heavy enough to support top-growth that is likely to be fairly heavy once the rose is mature. Light plastic containers are not generally suitable. If you have a balcony or roof garden where weight is a serious issue and you have to use plastic, secure the container to a wall or railings. For best results, use a heavy, loam-based, high-fertility compost (soil mix). Peat or coir-based composts are suitable, but difficult to re-wet if they dry out, so you will have to water the rose more often. You can replace up to half the compost with garden compost or leafmould (leaves that have been gathered and then left to break down for one or two years).

Pruning and training

Correct pruning and training result in a fan-shaped climber with plenty of new growth and a rich display of flowers.

The techniques involved in pruning and training climbing roses depend on the rose's habit of growth (see Growth habits and flower shapes), and the decorative purpose for which it is grown. While most will flower reasonably well without extensive pruning, sooner or later they are likely to develop into ungainly, congested plants that bloom only at the top, while bare wood accumulates around the base of the plant.

Pruning keeps the plant vigorous because it regularly stimulates the production of fresh, new growth that is always healthier than the old. Training the stems as close to the horizontal as possible thwarts the plant's natural inclination to grow upwards. It promotes the production of vigorous, upward-growing laterals along the stems and creates a plant that will smother itself in flowers each year. Climbing roses that are stiffly upright, however, may have to be trained in a fan shape.

You need to bear in mind a few basic principles. Pruning always

stimulates vigorous new growth. The harder you cut a shoot back, the more vigorously it will grow back. To promote even growth, prune the most vigorous stems lightly and weaker stems hard.

The timing of pruning depends on whether the rose flowers on the old or new wood. The majority of roses that flower only once a year (mostly ramblers) flower on wood that was produced the previous year, and some ramblers flower well on stems that are even older. Prune these roses immediately after their flowering season has finished.

Roses that flower twice or in succession (mostly climbers) flower on old and new wood, and are pruned during clear, dry (but not frosty) weather during the dormant period.

After any pruning, it is usually good practice to feed the plant in order to encourage vigour. However, if you prune in autumn or later, allow the rose to become dormant and delay feeding until growth emerges the following spring. Otherwise you may encourage sappy growth that does not have time to ripen before winter, and is prone to frost damage.

Burn all rose prunings. Do not shred them for use as compost, since they may harbour viruses.

■ BELOW
In a confined space, restrict the number of
main stems and train them in an S-shape.

Making the cuts

Secateurs are suitable for most rose
pruning, but for major tasks (see
Pruning a neglected climber) heavy-
duty long-handled pruners or a pruning
saw may be necessary. Use tools with
clean, sharp blades. Blunt or rusty
blades will snag the wood, providing
an entry point for disease. After use,
clean the blades with an oily rag.

New growth arises from the bud
nearest the cut. To ensure new stems
that can be trained horizontally,
prune to a bud facing in the direction
you wish the stem to grow (usually
outward-facing). Cut just above the
bud. If you cut too close to it, you
may damage it; too far away and
the stub of stem above the bud will
blacken and die back, providing an
entry point for disease.

Angle the secateurs so that the cut
slopes away from the bud. Rain will
then run off away from the bud,
rather than into it, where the water
might collect and cause rotting.

■ LEFT
INCORRECT *(left)*:
the stem on the left has
been cut too far away
from the emerging bud;
the one on the right has
been cut too close and the
bud has been damaged.

CORRECT *(right)*:
The clean cut, made
just above the bud, has
also been correctly angled
away from it to allow
rainwater to run off.

Formative pruning and training

On planting a climbing rose, no
pruning is necessary other than to
remove weak, twiggy growth and
dead or damaged wood.

In the first few years after planting,
keep pruning to a minimum to build
up the main framework of stems. This
is particularly important on sports of
bush roses, such as 'Climbing Blue
Moon', that can revert to the bush
form if cut back too hard.

To train a rose against a wall or
fence, tie the main shoots, loosely
with soft twine or horticultural string,
horizontally to the support. Where
the space is too narrow to accommo-
date the spread of the plant, train the
stems serpentine-fashion. Fewer main

PRUNING A NEGLECTED CLIMBER

2 Remove all the dead wood from the rose. Cut back old, dead stems to the base, and any other dead wood back to living wood.

3 Shorten healthy, vigorous stems that are too stiff to train in by about a half or more to encourage new growth from near the base.

1 This rose, the stiffly upright 'Handel', has not been pruned or trained properly. No system of wires or strings was established on the post for training the stems, and the rose has been allowed to grow upright, with the result that all the flowers are carried near the top. Though generally healthy, it is not realizing its flowering potential; dead wood has accumulated that can harbour disease and provide a nesting place for pests. Remedial action is required. (The pruning was carried out in autumn.)

4 For training the stems, knock in vine eyes about 45cm (18in) apart, and run lengths of string or galvanized or coated wire between them.

5 Tie in suitably placed stems, spiralling them around the post as far as is possible. Tie in loosely with wire or horticultural string.

■ RIGHT
A rose that is well pruned and trained will have a good covering of flowers.

6 *(left)* By reducing the amount of wood on the plant, you will encourage fresh new growth the following season. Spiral strong shoots around the post, and tie them in as they grow. This will encourage the production of flowering laterals from the base of the plant to the top.

stems will be needed, but the flowering display will be just as good.

On a pergola upright, attach narrow sections of trellis or wires running through vine eyes and tie the stems to these, training them spirally.

To train a rose against a tree, insert canes leading from the base of the rose to the tree trunk and tie the stems loosely to them (see Planting against a tree). Once the stems are long enough, wrap them around the trunk or one of the lower branches, tying them loosely to each other.

Pruning established roses

For roses that are grown as free-standing shrubs, pruning can be restricted to the routine removal of dead, diseased and damaged growth. Extensive pruning is not usually practical on roses that are grown into other plants. Any pruning necessary will be easiest when the rose is dormant in winter.

Guidelines for pruning more formally trained roses are as follows:

Climbing roses

Once the main framework is established, prune annually between autumn and early spring. Shorten any main shoots that have outgrown their space to an outward-facing bud.

Cut out any old stems that are no longer productive, and train in any vigorous new stems from the base as replacements. Shorten laterals by about two-thirds, cutting back to an outward-facing bud.

On older plants, if there is adequate new growth, cut back to the base all old main stems that have thickened and are no longer productive. If there are no suitable new stems, cut the old stems back to about 30–45cm (12–18in) above ground level. They should produce vigorous new shoots the following season (see also Renovative pruning).

On repeat-flowering roses, deadhead after the main flush to

encourage further flowers (see Dead-heading). After the second flush, shorten the flowered shoots again.

Rambling roses

Prune rambling roses in late summer after flowering. Ramblers flower well on wood over one year old, so you can restrict pruning to the removal of dead, diseased and damaged wood and shortening the flowered shoots (see Deadheading). Cut out older, less productive stems at the base, then pull them through the plant, or cut them into sections to remove them.

For a more compact plant, cut out all flowered stems at the base annually, and allow the vigorous new basal shoots to replace them.

DEADHEADING

Where roses bear their flowers in clusters, which is common to the majority of rambling roses, start deadheading by removing any individual faded flowers within the cluster. Single flowers can be removed as they fade.

Once the whole flower cluster has faded, cut back to a strong bud facing the way you wish the stem to grow. Here the leaves nearest the cluster are showing signs of black spot, so cut back to a bud behind the diseased growth.

RENOVATING A NEGLECTED CLIMBER

Deadheading

On repeat-flowering roses, remove dead flowers as they fade, to promote fresh blooms.

On roses that bear their flowers singly, cut back the stem to just above a bud facing the direction you wish it to grow. If the flowers are borne in clusters, cut just above a suitable growth bud to remove the whole cluster. Where the stems are trained horizontally, shorten the flowered laterals to two or three sets of leaves. On a large, mature rambler, clip over the whole plant with shears if you do not have time to remove the spent flowers individually.

Feed repeat-flowering roses after the first deadheading.

Where the spent flowers develop into eye-catching showy hips, deadheading is unnecessary.

Renovative pruning

You can rejuvenate a rose that has got out of hand with renovative pruning.

In winter or early spring, cut back all growth to about 30–45cm (12–18in) from the base. Vigorous new stems should emerge in spring. This drastic pruning is suitable for climbing roses that have retained a

1 This is a neglected climbing rose in need of renovative pruning.

2 Thick stems may require a pruning saw; single-edged ones are best.

3 Use long-handled pruners to cut back growth that is too thick for secateurs.

4 This shows how the rose looks after renovative pruning is complete.

good proportion of healthy growth, and is effective on nearly all ramblers.

On older plants that are less healthy and may die if ruthlessly cut back in one go, renovation should be staggered over two or three years. In year one, cut back one-third to a half of all stems to about 15–30cm (6–12in) from the base. The following year, provided new growth

has been produced from the base, cut back a half of all the remaining stems. Cut back the rest in the third year.

Feed, water and mulch the plant well after renovative pruning.

If the plant does not produce new growth from the base in the first year after drastic pruning, dig it up and burn it. Roses are unlikely to flower well the first summer after renovation.

Propagation

The majority of climbing roses are highly bred plants that can only be propagated by vegetative means. Only seed collected from species will yield new plants that are true to the parent. Cuttings are the easiest method of propagation for the amateur gardener, though they generally produce plants that are smaller than the parent. Commercial growers use budding, a technique that produces vigorous saleable plants more quickly.

Taking cuttings

Rose cuttings can be taken in summer (semi-ripe) or autumn (fully ripe or hardwood). Most gardeners prefer hardwood cuttings, as the aftercare required is minimal.

Hardwood cuttings

Take the cuttings in the autumn, after leaf-drop. They should be rooted by the following year. Transfer them to the garden if they are sufficiently developed; otherwise allow them to grow on *in situ* for another year.

Semi-ripe cuttings

In very cold areas you may have more success with semi-ripe cuttings, taken while the plants are still in active growth. Although these need more attention than hardwood cuttings,

1 Prepare a trench about 23–30cm (9–12in) deep in the open ground and line it to one-third of its depth with sharp sand to ensure that there is good drainage.

3 Dip the base of the cutting in hormone rooting powder and tap off the excess.

5 Firm the cuttings in and water them well. You may need to refirm them during the winter, if hard frosts cause the soil to heave and the cuttings to lift.

2 Cut well-ripened, pencil-thick stems from the rose, remove the soft tip and trim to a length of about 23cm (9in), making the base cut just below a leaf joint. Remove any remaining leaves.

4 Insert the cutting in the trench, leaving about 7.5cm (3in) above the soil surface.

with proper care a higher proportion is likely to root.

Select a side-shoot that is still green, but beginning to turn woody at the base, cutting just above an outward-facing bud. Trim the cutting at the base, just below a leaf joint, and cut back the soft tip to leave a stem about 10cm (4in) long.

Remove the lower leaves and all the thorns. Dip the base of the cutting in hormone rooting powder,

BUDDING

1 Cut a strong, ripe, healthy stem from the parent plant.

2 Trim off the leaves from the stem using sharp secateurs.

3 Snap off the thorns, wearing gloves to protect your hands if necessary.

4 Holding the stem with its growing point towards you, locate a dormant bud. Place the blade of the knife behind it, then draw it towards you, cutting beneath the bud.

5 Pull the knife through sharply to tear off a "tail" of bark (this is merely to help you handle the bud). Remove the woody pith behind the bud, using the knife if necessary.

6 Make a T-shaped cut in the rootstock, making sure that you cut no deeper than the bark. Ease back the bark from the cut using the tip of the knife.

7 Insert the bud in the cut with the tail uppermost.

8 Trim back the tail so that it is level with the top of the "T".

9 Bind the stem with a rubber tie and secure it with a pin. The rubber will stretch as the bud begins to swell and grow.

and insert it up to two-thirds of its length in a pot that contains a 50:50 mixture of peat and sharp sand.

Firm the cuttings in with your fingers, then spray with a solution of fungicide to moisten the compost and to kill off any fungal spores and bacteria. Label the cuttings, then tent the pot with a plastic bag to prevent moisture loss. Support the bag with canes or wire hoops to prevent any contact between the plastic and the leaves, since moisture will accumulate at that point and harbour bacteria.

Keep the cuttings in a shady, frost-free place. Regularly remove any fallen leaves and keep the rooting medium moist by watering with a fungicidal solution. Once the cuttings have rooted (usually the following spring), plant them out in a nursery bed to grow on for another year before planting out in their final position, or pot them up in loam-based compost (soil mix).

Budding

This is a technique that involves uniting material from the parent plant (the scion) with a strongly growing rootstock, usually of a species such as *Rosa multiflora* or *R. canina*. Rootstocks can sometimes be bought from commercial rose growers. Patient gardeners can raise their own rootstocks from seed.

Budding is usually carried out from mid-summer onwards while the plants are still growing. Choose a wet day, when the propagation material is less likely to dry out.

Select strong, healthy, well-ripened, non-flowering stems from the parent plant. To test the stems for ripeness, try bending one of the thorns. It should snap off cleanly.

If it is soft and flexible, the stem is not ripe enough.

Make sure that the knife you use is sharp and clean. Ragged cuts will not heal properly, and will provide an entry point for disease.

If the union between the rootstock and the scion takes, new growth will begin from the scion the following spring. You can then cut back the rootstock to just above the bud-graft. Leave the plant to develop *in situ* for at least a year before transferring it to its final position.

■ LEFT
If budding is successful, vigorous new growth will emerge in the spring.

Pests, diseases and other disorders

Most roses are prone to certain pests and diseases, but fortunately most of these are easy to control. Incidence of disease and pest attack is decided to some extent by the climate and regional variations. For example, black spot is more prevalent in some parts of the country than in others; powdery mildew is more likely to be a problem if the weather is hot and dry; and greenfly populations are governed in part by the winter survival of their predators.

Some rambling roses are prone to mildew after flowering, when they produce a mass of vigorous new shoots that can become congested. The problem is likely to be worse when they are grown against walls and air circulation is poor, but can be lessened by appropriate pruning (see Pruning and training).

Maintaining good standards of garden hygiene decreases the likelihood and the severity of many problems. Regularly clear up any plant debris, such as fallen leaves, which may rot and harbour disease both from the roses and from other plants. For the same reason you should burn, or dispose of, any rose prunings. (Do not use them for compost.)

Systemic insecticides and fungicides are applied as a spray and are absorbed by the plant. They do not kill the pest or disease directly, so their effect is not immediate. Repeated applications are usually necessary. Always follow the manufacturer's instructions.

Aphids

How to identify: The most common aphid to attack roses is greenfly. It is usually spotted near the start of the season on the ends of stems and developing flowerbuds.
Cause: Failure to destroy prunings from the previous season that may harbour eggs, though in practice this pest is virtually endemic and

Aphids (greenfly)

you are likely to encounter it every season.
Control: Spray the plants with a proprietary systemic insecticide as soon as you notice an infestation, and

repeat as directed by the manufacturer.

Some insecticides are specific to aphids and leave beneficial insects such as ladybirds unharmed. Though infestations may be heavy, the pest is easy to control and long-term damage can be avoided.

Balling

How to identify: Petals turn brown and cling together so that the flowers fail to open.
Cause: Prolonged wet weather while the buds are developing. Greenfly infestations earlier in the season can lead to balling.
Control: Not possible. Balling is a seasonal problem that does not affect the health of the plant overall, but you

Balling

should remove balled flowers that may otherwise rot and allow other diseases to take a hold on the plant.

Roses with very delicate petals are the most susceptible

to balling, but ensuring that they are planted where they will receive adequate sunlight and ventilation to dry the blooms will help minimize the risk of rain damage.

Black spot

How to identify: Black spots or patches develop on the leaves and, in some cases, the stems from mid-summer onwards. The leaves yellow and eventually drop off. Plants left untreated die back.
Cause: A bacterium that overwinters in the soil, then enters the plant during the growing season. Leaving infected prunings on the ground increases the likelihood of its occurrence.
Control: Remove all the

Black spot

infected leaves and stems and destroy them, then spray the plant with Bordeaux mixture. In severe cases it may be necessary to cut the plant back hard. Then feed and water it well in order to encourage recovery.

Black spot is more common in certain areas, and certain rose varieties are more susceptible to it than others. In severe cases, replace the plants with disease-resistant, guaranteed disease-free stock.

Powdery mildew

How to identify: A whitish-grey powder appears on the leaves and stems which, if left untreated, can cover the whole plant. It occurs from early summer onwards.
Cause: Various fungi that thrive in dry soil; they are most likely to cause damage where the air is stagnant.
Control: Spray with a proprietary fungicide.

Mildew

Prune rambling roses, which are particularly susceptible, in order to prevent congested growth and improve air circulation through the plant. Mulch well to conserve soil moisture. Avoid using high-nitrogen fertilizers.

Rust

How to identify: Orange spots that turn black appear on the undersides of leaves from mid-summer onwards. If left untreated, rust can be fatal.
Cause: Fungal spores that are more prevalent in humid weather.
Control: Remove infected parts of the plant, then spray with a fungicide.

Rust

Improve air circulation around the plants as for mildew.

Die back

How to identify: Flowerbuds, where present, fail to mature, and wither. Beginning at the tip of the stem, leaves begin to wither and drop off. The stem itself droops and may blacken.
Cause: Any of the diseases above, if not controlled, can lead to die back, but the condition may also be due to other fungi or bacteria, frost damage or a lack of soil nutrients, particularly potassium and phosphorus.
Control: Cut back all affected growth to healthy wood, then feed the plant. If die back

Die back

occurs in the autumn, do not feed until the spring, as any new growth that you promote will itself be susceptible to winter frost damage.

Proliferation

How to identify: The stem continues to grow through the open flower, producing a further bud or cluster of buds.
Cause: Damage to the stem while it is growing, either by frost or a virus.
How to control: Cut off affected stems. If only one or a few stems are affected, further steps are unnecessary, but where the whole plant has the condition, a virus is probably the culprit and the whole plant should be dug up and destroyed.

Proliferation

Rose-sick soil

How to identify: The roses suddenly fail to thrive, and begin to die back.
Cause: Unknown, but assumed to be a combination of nutrient exhaustion and fungal and bacterial activity in the soil. It often occurs in ground that has supported roses for a number of years.
How to control: Dig up and discard the roses, then replace the top 45cm (18in) of soil with fresh soil and replant the area with new stock, preferably a different type.

Rose-sick soil

Calendar

Early spring

Improve the soil and plant new stock. On established plants, cut out any dead, diseased or damaged wood. Fork rose fertilizer around the base as growth emerges, water in well and mulch. Cut back the rootstock on roses budded the previous summer that are showing signs of fresh growth. Renovate neglected plants (see Renovative pruning).

Mulching around the base of a rose conserves moisture in the soil and keeps down weeds.

Mid- to late spring

Check for and begin control of aphid infestations. Plant new stock.

Mid-summer

Deadhead repeat-flowering roses and feed with rose fertilizer. Shear over large ramblers. Increase your stock

Check your roses regularly. Pests and diseases can strike with alarming speed, so quick treatment is vital.

by taking semi-ripe cuttings or by budding. Check for and control black spot, rust and mildew. Plant new container-grown stock. Water roses in containers regularly, particularly in periods of drought.

Roses in containers will need regular watering throughout the summer, especially during hot, dry spells.

Late summer

Tie in strong new shoots to extend the framework. Continue to take semi-ripe cuttings of vigorous plants.

Semi-ripe cuttings, taken at the end of summer, are an easy way of increasing your supply of roses.

Autumn

Fork in bonemeal around the base of the plants, water in well and mulch. Plant new stock. Take hardwood cuttings of vigorous roses. Prune to remove all the old, unproductive wood, cutting back to the base where necessary.

An autumn feed of bonemeal promotes good root growth in climbing roses.

Other recommended climbing roses

As well as the roses illustrated in the Plant Directory, the following climbers and ramblers are recommended. The date of introduction follows the name of the rose in parentheses. Dimensions of the rose, given good growing conditions, are given at the end of the description, the first

'Bantry Bay'

figure indicating the rose's final height, the second its spread.

'Alister Stella Gray' (1894). Climbing rose with fully double, quartered rosette, fragrant yellow flowers from summer to autumn. 5m (16½ft) x 3m (10ft).

'Altissimo' (1966). Climbing rose with single, cupped, vivid red flowers from summer to autumn. 3m (10ft) x 2.4m (8ft).

R. banksiae 'Lutea' (1824). Climbing rose with clusters of small, very slightly scented, double yellow flowers in late

spring or early summer. 12m (40ft) x 6m (20ft).

'Bantry Bay' (1967). Climbing rose with clusters of cupped, semi-double, lightly scented, pale rose-pink flowers that open flat from summer to autumn. Glossy foliage. 4m (13ft) x 2.4m (8ft).

'Blush Rambler' (1903). Rambling rose of spreading habit with clusters of cupped, semi-double, scented, pale pink flowers in mid- to late summer. 4m (13ft) x 5m (16½ft).

'Céline Forestier' (1842). Climbing rose with rounded, double, quartered, fragrant creamy-yellow flowers from late spring to autumn. 2.4m (8ft) x 1.2m (4ft).

'City Girl' (1994). Climbing rose with semi-double, fragrant creamy-pink flowers from summer to autumn. 2.4m (8ft) x 2.4m (8ft).

'Climbing Etoile de Hollande' (1931). Climbing rose with cupped, double, fragrant, deep red flowers throughout summer. 6m (20ft) x 5m (16½ft).

'Climbing Lady Hillingdon' (1917). Climbing rose with double, sweetly scented, apricot-yellow flowers that open from pointed buds from summer to autumn. 5m (16½ft) x 2.4m (8ft).

'Climbing Masquerade' (1958). Climbing rose. From summer to autumn, clusters

of semi-double flowers open yellow, then change to pink and age to red, all colours appearing on the plant simultaneously. 2.4m (8ft) x 1.5m (5ft).

'Climbing Mrs Sam McGredy' (1937). Climbing rose with double, fragrant, copper-red flowers from

'Dreaming Spires'

mid-summer to autumn. 3m (10ft) x 3m (10ft).

'Climbing Orange Sunblaze' (1986). Miniature climbing rose with cupped, fully double, bright orange-red flowers from summer to autumn. 1.5m (5ft) x 1.2m (4ft).

'Climbing Shot Silk' (1931). Climbing rose with urn-shaped to cupped, fully double, heavily fragrant flowers that are pink overlaid with yellow and orange. 3m (10ft) x 2.4m (8ft).

'Copenhagen' (1964). Climbing rose with double,

fragrant, scarlet flowers in summer and autumn. 3m (10ft) x 1.5m (5ft).

'Crimson Shower' (1951). Climbing rose with clusters of rosette, double, bright red flowers from summer to autumn. Glossy foliage. 2.4m (8ft) x 2.1m (7ft).

'Della Balfour' (1994). Climbing rose with loosely double, fragrant, orange-yellow flowers from summer to autumn. 2.4m (8ft) x 1.8m (6ft).

'Dorothy Perkins' (1901). Rambling rose with clusters of scentless, double, rose-pink flowers appearing from late summer to autumn. 3m (10ft) x 3m (10ft).

'Dortmund' (1955). Climbing rose with single, bright red flowers with white eyes that open flat from summer to autumn. 3m (10ft) x 2m (6½ft).

'Dreaming Spires' (1973). Climbing rose with double, rounded, fragrant, rich yellow flowers from summer to autumn. 3m (10ft) x 2.1m (7ft).

'Easlea's Golden Rambler' (1932). Rambling rose with rounded, fully double, fragrant, apricot-yellow flowers that are marked with red in summer. 6m (20ft) x 5m (16½ft).

'Emily Gray' (1918). Rambling rose with clusters of rounded, fragrant, double, buff yellow flowers in summer. 5m (16½ft) x 3m (10ft).

'Excelsa' (1909). Climbing rose with clusters of rosette, double, red flowers in summer. 4m (13ft) x 3m (10ft).
'Félicité Perpétue' (1827). Rambling rose with rosette, fully double, fragrant, light pink to ivory white flowers in summer. 5m (16½ft) x 4m (13ft).
R. filipes 'Kiftsgate' (1954). Rambling rose with clusters of single, fragrant, white flowers in summer. Vigorous. 10m (33ft) x 6m (20ft).
'François Juranville' (1906). Rambling rose with rosette, fully double, fragrant, pale salmon-pink flowers in summer. Prone to mildew when grown against a wall. 6m (20ft) x 5m (16½ft).
'Galway Bay' (1966). Climbing rose with large, double, rich pink flowers from summer to autumn. 3m (10ft) x 1.8m (6ft).
'Goldfinch' (1907). Rambling rose with rosette, double, scented, deep yellow flowers, fading to pale cream in summer. 2.4m (8ft) x 2m (6½ft).
'Good as Gold' (1995). Miniature climbing rose with small, double, fragrant, bright yellow flowers from summer to autumn. 2m (6½ft) x 1.5m (5ft).
'Guinée' (1938). Climbing rose with cupped, fully double, fragrant, dark red flowers in summer. 5m (16½ft) x 2.1m (7ft).
'Hamburger Phoenix' (1954).

Climbing rose with semi-double, slightly fragrant, deep red flowers that open flat in summer and autumn. 3m (10ft) x 1.5m (5ft).
'High Hopes' (1992). Climbing rose with double, fragrant, light pink flowers from summer to autumn. 4m (13ft) x 2.4m (8ft).

'Climbing Shot Silk'

'Leaping Salmon' (1986). Climbing rose with double, urn-shaped, fragrant, pink flowers in summer and autumn. 3m (10ft) x 1.8m (6ft).
'Leverkusen' (1954). Climbing rose with clusters of double, slightly fragrant, light yellow flowers from summer to autumn. Glossy foliage. 3m (10ft) x 2.1m (7ft).
'Little Rambler' (1994). Rambling rose with clusters of small, fully double, scented, pale pink flowers in summer. 2.1m (7ft) x 2.1m (7ft).
'Meg' (1954). Climbing rose

with clusters of large, semi-double, fragrant, warm pink flowers that open flat from summer to autumn. 4m (13ft) x 4m (13ft).
R. mulliganii (1919). Rambling species rose with large clusters of single, delicately scented, white flowers in summer; vigorous. 6m (20ft) x 3m (10ft).
'New Dawn' (1930). Climbing rose with clusters of cupped, fully double, fragrant, shell-pink flowers that fade to white from summer to autumn. Striking glossy foliage. 3m (10ft) x 2.4m (8ft).
'Night Light' (1982). Climbing rose with double, rounded, fragrant, yellow flowers, summer to autumn. 2.4m (8ft) x 2.1m (7ft).
'Paul's Himalayan Musk' (1916). Rambling rose with clusters of rosette, double, fragrant, pink flowers in summer. 10m (33ft) x 10m (33ft).
'Paul's Lemon Pillar' (1915). Climbing rose with shapely, fully double, scented, creamy white flowers in summer. 4m (13ft) x 3m (10ft).
'Paul's Scarlet Climber' (1915). Climbing rose with clusters of cupped, double, virtually scentless, bright red flowers that gradually age to purplish-grey in summer. 3m (10ft) x 3m (10ft).
'Phyllis Bide' (1923). Climbing rose with clusters of

rosette, double, lightly scented, apricot-pink flowers from summer to autumn. Small leaves. 2.4m (8ft) x 1.5m (5ft).
'Ramona' (1913). Climbing rose with single, virtually scentless, intense red flowers that open flat to reveal golden stamens in early summer. 2.4m (8ft) x 3m (10ft).

'American Pillar'

'Ritter von Barmstede' (1960). Climbing rose with large clusters of small, double, slightly fragrant, deep pink flowers in summer and autumn. 3m (10ft) x 1.5m (5ft).
'Rosy Mantle' (1968). Climbing rose with fully double, fragrant, deep rose-pink flowers from summer to autumn. 2.4m (8ft)x 2m (6½ft).
'Royal Gold' (1957). Climbing rose with double, slightly fragrant, deep yellow flowers in summer and autumn. Slightly tender. 2.4m (8ft) x 1.2m (4ft).

Index

ACKNOWLEDGEMENTS

The publisher would like to thank the following for their help in the production of this book: Cants of Colchester, Colchester; Gandy's Roses Ltd, North Kilworth, Leics; Mattock's Roses, Nuneham Courtenay, Oxon; Mr and Mrs A. Keech, Long Buckby, Northants; Mr and Mrs A. Shepherd, Long Buckby, Northants; Mrs Ann Hartley, Long Buckby, Northants; Rearsby Roses, Rearsby, Leics; Royal National Rose Society, St Albans, Herts; The Hon. and Mrs Simon Howard, Castle Howard, Yorkshire. We would also like to thank: Peter McHoy for loaning the pictures on pages 9, 13r, 42, 44r (t and b), 50, 60br, 61l, 61r, 62l, 62r and 63l; and The Harpur Garden Picture Library for the pictures on pages 2 (de Bunsen), 6–7 (Fudler's Hall, Chelmsford), 13l, 14l (Design: Tessa Hobbs) and 15 (Stellenberg).